Thank you for

with us during

R.I.C. Melbourne.

May '93.

11/55 CANTERBURY Rd.
MIDDLE PARK
VIC 3206.

AUSTRALIA.

EMERALD HILL BOOKSHOP
699-5966

BANJO PATERSON
Favourite Poems

BANJO PATERSON
Favourite Poems

Illustrated with Australian Landscape Paintings

Selected by Margaret Olds

Sydney:
THE CARMEL PRESS

Published by
The Carmel Press
an imprint of Murray Child & Company Pty Ltd
64 Suffolk Avenue, Collaroy Plateau, NSW, Australia, 2098
First Edition 1992
This collection of poems and paintings
© Murray Child & Company Pty Ltd 1992
© Design, Murray Child & Company Pty Ltd 1992
This book has been edited, designed, typeset and electronically
composed in Australia by the publisher
Typesetting processed by Deblaere Typesetting Pty Ltd
Printed in Singapore by Colourwork Press Pte Ltd

National Library of Australia
Cataloguing-in-Publication data

Paterson, A.B. (Andrew Barton), 1864–1941.
Banjo Paterson favourite poems.

ISBN 0 908048 12 2.

I. Olds, Margaret. II Title. III. Title: Favourite poems.

A821.2

Contents

Introduction

A. B. ("Banjo") Paterson was born on 17 February 1864 on Narambla Station near Orange. He spent his early childhood in the bush, growing up on Illalong Station near Yass. Here he learned to ride, met a variety of bush characters and discovered a lot about life in the bush which stood him in good stead in his later years.

While he was being educated at Sydney Grammar School Paterson lived with his grandmother, Emily Barton, at Gladesville. She wrote poetry herself and had a considerable influence over the young boy. Following his matriculation at the age of sixteen, he was articled to a Sydney lawyer's office where he qualified as a solicitor.

He started writing poetry late in the 1880s while working in the law and was successfully published in the *Bulletin* under the name of "The Banjo". One of his enduring classics, "Clancy of the Overflow", was published in 1889. In 1895 "Waltzing Matilda" was written. In the same year, *The Man from Snowy River and Other Verses* was published by Angus & Robertson to instant acclaim. This volume was reprinted four times in six months and is still the most successful volume of Australian poetry ever published.

In 1898 Paterson went to South Africa as a war correspondent to cover the Boer War and later travelled to China to report on the Boxer Rebellion. He left the law in 1900 to work as a journalist with the *Sydney Morning Herald* and went on to become editor of the Sydney *Evening News* and later the *Australian Town and Country Journal*. From 1900 onwards he successfully combined the two careers of journalist and poet. In 1902 his second book of verse, *Rio Grande's Last Race and Other Verses,* was published. Late in this decade he bought a property on the upper Murrumbidgee and again lived in the bush.

Soon after the outbreak of the First World War Paterson went to

London hoping to become a war correspondent but was unable to get to the Front in France. Dissatisifed with this, he returned to Australia where he joined the Remount Service which provided horses for Australia's cavalry in the Middle East.

His third book of poems, *Saltbush Bill J.P. and Other Verses*, was published during the war in 1917. After the war Paterson returned to the upper Murrumbidgee, but then lived in Sydney from 1919 onwards. He continued to publish verse, short stories, children's poems and longer fiction into the 1930s. He died in Sydney in February 1941.

In total his work includes three books of verse, a children's book, two novels, a book of short stories, a semi-autobiographical collection and the first anthology of Australian bush songs. However, he is best remembered for his poetry.

Paterson is Australia's best known folk poet and myth maker. "The Man from Snowy River", "Waltzing Matilda" and "Clancy of the Overflow" are outstanding examples of his skill which have drawn a huge response from generations of Australians. Paterson's ability to capture the essence of Australia and touch the imagination of today's Australians is shown in the continuing popularity of his work and also in the success of the Australian movie, *The Man from Snowy River.*

The paintings which accompany this selection were chosen to complement the poems. They are among Australia's best known and best loved works from the brushes of such painters as Tom Roberts, Frederick McCubbin, Sir Arthur Streeton and Hans Heysen. Like the poems, these paintings from Paterson's time present a uniquely Australian view of our country and the way our forebears lived, worked and played.

Margaret Olds

Shearing
at Castlereagh

Tom Roberts, 1856–1931, Australian,
Shearing the Rams, 1890, oil on canvas
(lined onto board), 121.9 x 182.6 cm. Felton
Bequest 1932. National Gallery of Victoria.

The bell is set aringing, and the engine gives a toot,
There's five and thirty shearers here are shearing for the loot,
So stir yourselves, you penners-up and shove the sheep along,
The musterers are fetching them a hundred thousand strong,
And make your collie dogs speak up—what would the buyers say
In London if the wool was late this year from Castlereagh?

8

The man that "rung" the Tubbo shed is not the ringer here,
That stripling from the Cooma side can teach him how to shear.
They trim away the ragged locks, and rip the cutter goes,
And leaves a track of snowy fleece from brisket to the nose;
It's lovely how they peel it off with never stop nor stay,
They're racing for the ringer's place this year at Castlereagh.

The man that keeps the cutters sharp is growling in his cage,
He's always in a hurry and he's always in a rage—
"You clumsy-fisted muttonheads, you'd turn a fellow sick,
You pass yourselves as shearers? You were born to swing a pick!
Another broken cutter here, that's two you've broke today,
It's awful how such crawlers come to shear at Castlereagh."

The youngsters picking up the fleece enjoy the merry din,
They throw the classer up the fleece, he throws it to the bin;
The pressers standing by the rack are waiting for the wool,
There's room for just a couple more, the press is nearly full;
Now jump upon the lever, lads, and heave and heave away,
Another bale of golden fleece is branded "Castlereagh".

The Road to Hogan's Gap

Now look, y' see, it's this way like,
    Y' cross the broken bridge
And run the crick down till y' strike
    The second right-hand ridge.

The track is hard to see in parts,
    But still it's pretty clear;
There's been two Injin hawkers' carts
    Along that road this year.

Well, run that right-hand ridge along,
    It ain't, to say, too steep.
There's two fresh tracks might put y' wrong
    Where blokes went out with sheep.

But keep the crick upon your right,
    And follow pretty straight
Along the spur, until y' sight
    A wire and sapling gate.

Well, that's where Hogan's old grey mare
    Fell off and broke her back;
You'll see her carcase layin' there,
    Jist down below the track.

And then you drop two mile, or three,
    It's pretty steep and blind;
You want to go and fall a tree
    And tie it on behind.

And then you'll pass a broken cart
    Below a granite bluff;
And that is where you strike the part
    They reckon pretty rough.

But by the time you've got that far
    It's either cure or kill,
So turn your horses round the spur
    And face 'em up the hill.

For, look, if you should miss the slope
    And get below the track,
You haven't got the whitest hope
    Of ever gettin' back.

An' halfway up you'll see the hide
    Of Hogan's brindled bull;
Well, mind and keep the right-hand side,
    The left's too steep a pull

And both the banks is full of cracks;
    An' just about at dark
You'll see the last year's bullock tracks
    Where Hogan drew the bark.

The marks is old and pretty faint
    And grown with scrub and such;
Of course the track to Hogan's ain't
    A road that's travelled much.

But turn and run the tracks along
    For half a mile of more,
And then, of course, you can't go wrong—
    You're right at Hogan's door.

When first you come to Hogan's gate
    He mightn't show, perhaps;
He's pretty sure to plant and wait
    To see it ain't the traps.

I wouldn't call it good enough
    To let your horses out;
There's some that's pretty extra rough
    Is livin' round about.

It's likely if your horses did
    Get feedin' near the track,
It's goin' to cost at least a quid
    Or more to get them back.

Arthur Streeton, Australia, 1867–1943, *The selector's hut: Whelan on the log,* 1890, oil on canvas 76.7 x 51.2 cm. Collection: Australian National Gallery, Canberra. Reproduced with the kind permission of Mrs M. H. Streeton.

13

So, if you find they're off the place,
    It's up to you to go
And flash a quid in Hogan's face—
    He'll know the blokes that know.

But, listen, if you're feelin' dry,
    Just see there's no one near,
And go and wink the other eye
    And ask for ginger beer.

The blokes come in from near and far
    To sample Hogan's pop;
They reckon once they breast the bar
    They stay there till they drop.

On Sundays you can see them spread
    Like flies around the tap.
It's like that song "The Livin' Dead"
    Up there at Hogan's Gap.

They like to make it pretty strong
    Whenever there's a charnce;
So when a stranger comes along
    They always holds a darnce.

There's recitations, songs, and fights,
    They do the thing a treat.
There's one long bloke up there recites
    As well as e'er you'd meet.

They're lively blokes all right up there,
    It's never dull a day.
I'd go meself if I could spare
    The time to get away.

*   *   *

The stranger turned his horses, quick,
   He didn't cross the bridge.
He didn't go along the crick
   To strike the second ridge.

He didn't make the trip, because
   He wasn't feeling fit.
His business up at Hogan's was
   To serve him with a writ.

He reckoned if he faced the pull
   And climbed the rocky stair,
The next to come might find his hide
   A landmark on the mountain side,
Along with Hogan's brindled bull
   And Hogan's old grey mare!

The Swagman's Rest

We buried old Bob where the bloodwoods wave
    At the foot of the Eaglehawk;
We fashioned a cross on the old man's grave,
    For fear that his ghost might walk;
We carved his name on a bloodwood tree,
    With the date of his sad decease,
And in place of "Died from effects of spree",
    We wrote, "May he rest in peace".

For Bob was known on the Overland,
    A regular old bush wag,
Tramping along in the dust and sand,
    Humping his well worn swag.
He would camp for days in the river bed,
    And loiter and "fish for whales".
"I'm into the swagman's yard", he said,
    "And I never shall find the rails."

But he found the rails on that summer night
    For a better place—or worse,
As we watched by turns in the flickering light
    With an old black gin for nurse.
The breeze came in with the scent of pine,
    The river sounded clear,
When a change came on, and we saw the sign
    That told us the end was near.

But he spoke in a cultured voice and low—
    "I fancy they've 'sent the route';
I once was an army man, you know,
    Though now I'm a drunken brute;
But bury me out where the bloodwoods wave,
      And if ever you're fairly stuck,

Gordon Coutts, Australia, (c.1869)–1937, *Landscape with swagman*, 1889, oil on canvas, 35.6 x 45.7 cm. Art Gallery of New South Wales. Purchased 1956.

Just shovel me out of the grave,
  And, maybe, I'll bring you luck.

"For I've always heard—" here his voice fell weak,
  His strength was well-nigh sped,
He gasped and struggled and tried to speak,
  Then fell in a moment—dead.
Thus ended a wasted life and hard,
  Of energies misapplied—
Old Bob was out of the "swagman's yard"
  And over the Great Divide.

* * *

The drought came down on the field and flock,
  And never a raindrop fell,
Though the tortured moans of the starving stock
  Might soften a fiend from hell.
And we thought of the hint that the swagman gave
  When he went to the Great Unseen—
We shovelled the skeleton out of the grave
  To see what his hint might mean.

We dug where the cross and the graveposts were,
  We shovelled away the mould,
When sudden a vein of quartz lay bare
  All gleaming with yellow gold.
'Twas a reef with never a fault nor baulk
  That ran from the range's crest,
And the richest mine on the Eaglehawk
  Is known as "The Swagman's Rest".

Clancy of The Overflow

I had written him a letter which I had, for want of better
  Knowledge, sent to where I met him down the Lachlan, years ago;
He was shearing when I knew him, so I sent the letter to him,
  Just "on spec", addressed as follows: "Clancy, of The Overflow".

And an answer came directed in a writing unexpected,
  (And I think the same was written with a thumbnail dipped in tar);

William C. Piguenit, Australia, 1836–1914, *The flood on the Darling 1890* (1895), oil on canvas 122.5 x 199.3 cm. Art Gallery of New South Wales. Purchased 1895.

'Twas his shearing mate who wrote it, and *verbatim* I will quote it:
    "Clancy's gone to Queensland droving, and we don't know where he are."

*   *   *

In my wild erratic fancy visions come to me of Clancy
    Gone a-droving "down the Cooper" where the Western drovers go;
As the stock are slowly stringing, Clancy rides behind them singing,
    For the drover's life has pleasures that the townsfolk never know.

And the bush hath friends to meet him, and their kindly voices greet him
    In the murmur of the breezes and the river on its bars,
And he sees the vision splendid of the sunlit plains extended,
    And at night the wondrous glory of the everlasting stars.

*   *   *

I am sitting in my dingy little office, where a stingy
    Ray of sunlight struggles feebly down between the houses tall,

And the foetid air and gritty of the dusty, dirty city
   Through the open window floating, spreads its foulness over all.

And in place of lowing cattle, I can hear the fiendish rattle
   Of the tramways and the buses making hurry down the street,
And the language uninviting of the gutter children fighting,
   Comes fitfully and faintly through the ceaseless tramp of feet.

And the hurrying people daunt me, and their pallid faces haunt me
   As they shoulder one another in their rush and nervous haste,
With their eager eyes and greedy, and their stunted forms and weedy,
   For townsfolk have no time to grow, they have no time to waste.

And I somehow rather fancy that I'd like to change with Clancy,
   Like to take a turn at droving where the seasons come and go,
While he faced the round eternal of the cashbook and the journal—
   But I doubt he'd suit the office, Clancy, of "The Overflow".

Pioneers

They came of bold and roving stock that would not fixed abide;
They were the sons of field and flock since e'er they learned to ride;
We may not hope to see such men in these degenerate years
As those explorers of the bush—the brave old pioneers.

Robert Havell after William Light, *A view of the country and temporary erections near the site for the proposed town of Adelaide,* (c1835), engraving, hand coloured, sheet 57.5 x 73.2 cm. L.J. Wilson Bequest Fund, 1983. Collection: City of Ballaarat Fine Art Gallery.

'Twas they who rode the trackless bush in heat and storm and
    drought;
'Twas they that heard the master-word that called them further out;
'Twas they that followed up the trail the mountain cattle made
And pressed across the mighty range where now their bones are laid.

But now the times are dull and slow, the brave old days are dead
When hardy bushmen started out, and forced their way ahead
By tangled scrub and forests grim towards the unknown west,
And spied the far-off promised land from off the ranges' crest.

Oh! ye, that sleep in lonely graves by far-off ridge and plain,
We drink to you in silence now as Christmas comes again,
The men who fought the wilderness through rough, unsettled years—
The founders of our nation's life, the brave old pioneers.

Saltbush Bill

Now this is the law of the Overland that all in the West obey,
A man must cover with travelling sheep a six-mile stage a day;
But this is the law which the drovers make, right easily understood,
They travel their stage where the grass is bad, but they camp where
   the grass is good;
They camp, and they ravage the squatter's grass till never a blade remain.
Then they drift away as the white clouds drift on the edge of the saltbush
   plains,
From camp to camp and from run to run they battle it hand to hand,
For a blade of grass and the right to pass on the track of the Overland.

For this is the law of the Great Stock Routes, 'tis written in white and
   black—
The man that goes with a travelling mob must keep to a half-mile track;
And the drovers keep to a half-mile track on the runs where the grass is
   dead,
But they spread their sheep on a well-grassed run till they go with a two-
   mile spread.
So the squatters hurry the drovers on from dawn till the fall of night,
And the squatters' dogs and the drovers' dogs get mixed in a deadly
   fight;
Yet the squatters' men, though they hunt the mob, are willing the peace
   to keep,
For the drovers learn how to use their hands when they go with the
   travelling sheep;
But this is the tale of a Jackaroo that came from a foreign strand,
And the fight that he fought with Saltbush Bill, the King of the Overland

Now Saltbush Bill was a drover tough, as ever the country knew,
He had fought his way on the Great Stock Routes from the sea to the Big
   Barcoo;
He could tell when he came to a friendly run that gave him a chance to
   spread,

And he knew where the hungry owners were that hurried his sheep
    ahead;
He was drifting down in the Eighty drought with a mob that could
    scarcely creep,
(When the kangaroos by the thousands starve, it is rough on the travelling
    sheep.)
And he camped one night at the crossing place on the edge of the Wilga
    run,
"We must manage a feed for them here," he said, "or the half of the mob
    are done!"
So he spread them out when they left the camp wherever they liked to go,
Till he grew aware of a Jackaroo with a station hand in tow,
And they set to work on the straggling sheep, and with many a stockwhip
    crack
They forced them in where the grass was dead in the space of the half-
    mile track;
So William prayed that the hand of fate might suddenly strike him blue
But he'd get some grass for his starving sheep in the teeth of that
    Jackaroo.
So he turned and he cursed the Jackaroo, he cursed him alive or dead,
From the soles of his great unwieldy feet to the crown of his ugly head,
With an extra curse on the moke he rode and the cur at his heels that ran,
Till the Jackaroo from his horse got down and he went for the drover
    man;
With the station hand for his picker-up, though the sheep ran loose the
    while,
They battled it out on the saltbush plain in the regular prize ring style.

Now, the new chum fought for his honour's sake and the pride of the
    English race,
But the drover fought for his daily bread with a smile on his bearded face;
So he shifted ground and he sparred for wind and he made it a lengthy mill,
And from time to time as his scouts came in they whispered to Saltbush
    Bill—

Tom Roberts, Australia, 1856–1931, *A break away!* 1891,
Corowa, New South Wales and Melbourne, oil on canvas. 137.2
x 168.1 cm. Art Gallery of South Australia, Adelaide. Elder
Bequest Fund 1899.

"We have spread the sheep with a two-mile
    spread, and the grass it is something grand,
You must stick to him, Bill, for another round
    for the pride of the Overland."

The new chum made it a rushing fight, though
    never a blow got home,
Till the sun rode in the cloudless sky and glared
    on the brick-red loam,
Till the sheep drew in to the shelter trees and
    settled them down to rest,
Then the drover said he would fight no more and
    he gave his opponent best.
So the new chum rode to the homestead
    straight and he told them a story grand
Of the desperate fight that he fought that day
    with the King of the Overland.
And the tale went home to the public schools of the pluck of the English
    swell,
How the drover fought for his very life, but blood in the end must tell.
But the travelling sheep and the Wilga sheep were boxed on the Old
    Man Plain.
'Twas a full week's work ere they drafted out and hunted them off again,

With a week's good grass in their wretched hides, with a curse and a stockwhip crack,
They hunted them off on the road once more to starve on the half-mile track.
And Saltbush Bill, on the Overland, will many a time recite
How the best day's work that ever he did was the day that he lost the fight.

With the Cattle

The drought is down on field and flock,
 The river bed is dry;
And we must shift the starving stock
 Before the cattle die.
We muster up with weary hearts
 At breaking of the day,
And turn our heads to foreign parts,
 To take the stock away.
   And it's hunt 'em up and dog 'em,
   And it's get the whip and flog 'em,
For it's weary work is droving when they're dying every day;
   By stock routes bare and eaten,
   On dusty roads and beaten,
With half a chance to save their lives we take the stock away.

We cannot use the whip for shame
 On beasts that crawl along;
We have to drop the weak and lame,
 And try to save the strong;
The wrath of God is on the track,
 The drought fiend holds his sway,
With blows and cries and stockwhip crack
 We take the stock away.
   As they fall we leave them lying,
   With the crows to watch them dying,
Grim sextons of the Overland that fasten on their prey;
   By the fiery dust storm drifting,
   And the mocking mirage shifting,
In heat and drought and hopeless pain we take the stock away.

In dull despair the days go by
 With never hope of change,
But every stage we draw more nigh

26

Hans Heysen, Australia, 1877–1968, *Mystic Morn*, 1904, oil on canvas 122.5 x 184 cm. Art Gallery of South Australia, Adelaide. Elder Bequest Fund 1939.

Towards the mountain range;
And some may live to climb the pass,
   And reach the great plateau,
And revel in the mountain grass,
   By streamlets fed with snow.
      As the mountain wind is blowing
      It starts the cattle lowing,
And calling to each other down the dusty long array;
      And there speaks a grizzled drover:
      "Well, thank God, the worst is over,
The creatures smell the mountain grass that's twenty miles away."

They press towards the mountain grass,
   They look with eager eyes
Along the rugged stony pass,
   That slopes towards the skies;
Their feet may bleed from rocks and stones,

But though the blood-drop starts,
They struggle on with stifled groans,
    For hope is in their hearts.
        And the cattle that are leading,
        Though their feet are worn and bleeding,
Are breaking to a kind of run—pull up, and let them go!
        For the mountain wind is blowing,
        And the mountain grass is growing,
They settle down by running streams ice-cold with melted snow.

The days are done of heat and drought
    Upon the stricken plain;
The wind has shifted right about,
    And brought the welcome rain;
The river runs with sullen roar,
    All flecked with yellow foam,
And we must take the road once more,
    To bring the cattle home.
        And it's "Lads! we'll raise a chorus,
        There's a pleasant trip before us."
And the horses bound beneath us as we start them down the track;
        And the drovers canter, singing,
        Through the sweet green grasses springing,
Towards the far-off mountain land, to bring the cattle back.

Are these the beasts we brought away
    That move so lively now?
They scatter off like flying spray
    Across the mountain's brow;
And dashing down the rugged range
    We hear the stockwhip crack,
Good faith, it is a welcome change
    To bring such cattle back.
        And it's "Steady down the lead there!"

And it's "Let 'em stop and feed there!"
For they're wild as mountain eagles and their sides are all afoam;
      But they're settling down already,
      And they'll travel nice and steady,
With cheery call and jest and song we fetch the cattle home.

We have to watch them close at night
    For fear they'll make a rush,
And break away in headlong flight
    Across the open bush;
And by the campfire's cheery blaze,
    With mellow voice and strong,
We hear the lonely watchman raise
    The Overlander's song:
      "Oh! it's when we're done with roving,
      With the camping and the droving,
It's homeward down the Bland we'll go, and never more we'll roam";
      While the stars shine out above us,
      Like the eyes of those who love us—
The eyes of those who watch and wait to greet the cattle home.

The plains are all awave with grass,
    The skies are deepest blue;
And leisurely the cattle pass
    And feed the long day through;
But when we sight the station gate,
    We make the stockwhips crack,
A welcome sound to those who wait
    To greet the cattle back:
      And through the twilight falling
      We hear their voices calling,
As the cattle splash across the ford and churn it into foam;
      And the children run to meet us,
      And our wives and sweethearts greet us,
Their heroes from the Overland who brought the cattle home.

The Daylight is Dying

The daylight is dying
 Away in the west,
The wild birds are flying
 In silence to rest;
In leafage and frondage
 Where shadows are deep,
They pass to its bondage—
 The kingdom of sleep.
And watched in their sleeping
 By stars in the height,
They rest in your keeping,
 Oh, wonderful night.

When night doth her glories
 Of starshine unfold,
'Tis then that the stories
 Of bushland are told.
Unnumbered I hold them
 In memories bright,
But who could unfold them,
 Or read them aright?
Beyond all denials
 The stars in their glories
The breeze in the myalls
 Are part of these stories.
The waving of grasses,
 The song of the river
That sings as it passes
 For ever and ever,
The hobble chains rattle,
 The calling of birds,

The lowing of cattle
 Must blend with the words.
Without these, indeed, you
 Would find it ere long,
As though I should read you
 The words of a song
That lamely would linger
 When lacking the rune,
The voice of the singer,
 The lilt of the tune.

Frederick McCubbin, *Winter Evening, Hawthorn*, 1886. Castlemaine Art Gallery and Historical Museum.

But, as one half-hearing
  An old-time refrain,
With memory clearing,
  Recalls it again,
These tales, roughly wrought of
  The bush and its ways,
May call back a thought of
  The wandering days,

And, blending with each
  In the mem'ries that throng,
There haply shall reach
  You some echo of song.

31

A Bushman's Song

I'm travellin' down the Castlereagh, and I'm a station hand,
I'm handy with the ropin' pole, I'm handy with the brand,
And I can ride a rowdy colt, or swing the axe all day,
But there's no demand for a station hand along the Castlereagh.

So it's shift, boys, shift, for there isn't the slightest doubt
That we've got to make a shift to the stations further out
With the packhorse runnin' after, for he follows like a dog,
We must strike across the country at the old jig-jog.

This old black horse I'm riding—if you'll notice what's his brand,
He wears the crooked R, you see—none better in the land.
He takes a lot of beating', and the other day we tried,
For a bit of a joke, with a racing bloke, for twenty pounds aside.

It was shift, boys, shift, for there wasn't the slightest doubt,
That I had to make him shift, for the money was nearly out;
But he cantered home a winner, with the other one at the flog—
He's a red-hot sort to pick up with his old jig-jog.

I asked a cove for shearin' once along the Marthaguy:
"We shear non-union here," says he. "I call it scab," says I.
I looked along the shearin' floor before I turned to go—
There were eight or ten dashed Chinamen a-shearin' in a row.

It was shift, boys, shift, for there wasn't the slightest doubt
It was time to make a shift with the leprosy about.
So I saddled up my horses, and I whistled to my dog,
And I left his scabby station at the old jig-jog.

I went to Illawarra where my brother's got a farm,
He has to ask his landlord's leave before he lifts his arm;

Charles Conder, 1868–1909, Australian, *Yarding Sheep*, 1890, oil on canvas 35.5 x 56 cm.
Bequeathed by Mrs Mary Helen Keep, 1944. National Gallery of Victoria, Melbourne.

The landlord owns the countryside—man, woman, dog, and cat,
They haven't the cheek to dare to speak without they touch their hat.

It was shift, boys, shift, for there wasn't the slightest doubt
Their little landlord god and I would soon have fallen out;
Was I to touch my hat to him?—was I his bloomin' dog?
So I makes for up the country at the old jig-jog.

But it's time that I was movin', I've a mighty way to go
Till I drink artesian water from a thousand feet below;
Till I meet the overlanders with the cattle comin' down,
And I'll work a while till I make a pile, then have a spree in town.

So, it's shift, boys, shift, for there isn't the slightest doubt
We've got to make a shift to the stations further out;
The packhorse runs behind us, for he follows like a dog,
And we cross a lot of country at the old jig-jog.

Father Riley's Horse

'Twas the horse thief, Andy Regan, that was hunted like a dog
    By the troopers of the upper Murray side,
They had searched in every gully—they had looked in every log,
    But never a sight or track of him they spied,
Till the priest at Kiley's Crossing heard a knocking very late
    And a whisper "Father Riley—come across!"
So his Rev'rence in pyjamas trotted softly to the gate
    And admitted Andy Regan—and a horse!

"Now, it's listen, Father Riley, to the words I've got to say,
    For it's close upon my death I am tonight.
With the troopers hard behind me I've been hiding out all day
    In the gullies keeping close and out of sight.
But they're watching all the ranges till there's not a bird could fly,
    And I'm fairly worn to pieces with the strife,
So I'm taking no more trouble, but I'm going home to die,
    'Tis the only way I see to save my life.

"Yes, I'm making home to mother's and I'll die o' Tuesday next
    An' be buried on the Thursday—and, of course,
I'm prepared to meet my penance, but with one thing I'm perplexed
    And it's—Father, it's this jewel of a horse!
He was never bought nor paid for, and there's not a man can swear
    To his owner or his breeder, but I know,
That his sire was by Pedantic from the Old Pretender mare
    And his dam was close related to The Roe.

"And there's nothing in the district that can race him for a step,
    He could canter while they're going at their top:
He's the king of all the leppers that was ever seen to lep,
    A five-foot fence—he'd clear it in a hop!
So I'll leave him with you, Father, till the dead shall rise again,
    'Tis yourself that knows a good 'un; and, of course,

George Rowe, *Victorian Race Meeting near Sunbury*, 1858, watercolour 67.9 x 167.6 cm. Dixson Galleries, Mitchell Library, Sydney.

You can say he's got by Moonlight out of Paddy Murphy's plain
    If you're ever asked the breeding of the horse!

"But it's getting on to daylight and it's time to say goodbye,
    For the stars above the east are growing pale.
And I'm making home to mother—and it's hard for me to die!
    But it's harder still, is keeping out of gaol!
You can ride the old horse over to my grave across the dip
    Where the wattle bloom is waving overhead.
Sure he'll jump them fences easy—you must never raise the whip
    Or he'll rush 'em—now, goodbye!" and he had fled!

So they buried Andy Regan, and they buried him to rights,
    In the graveyard at the back of Kiley's Hill;
There were five-and-twenty mourners who had five-and-twenty fights
    Till the very boldest fighters had their fill.
There were fifty horses racing from the graveyard to the pub,
    And the riders flogged each other all the while.
And the lashin's of the liquor! And the lavin's of the grub!
    Oh, poor Andy went to rest in proper style.

Then the races came to Kiley's—with a steeplechase and all,
    For the folk were mostly Irish round about,
And it takes an Irish rider to be fearless of a fall,

They were training morning in and morning out.
But they never started training till the sun was on the course
    For superstitious story kept 'em back,
That the ghost of Andy Regan on a slashing chestnut horse,
    Had been training by the starlight on the track.

And they read the nominations for the races with surprise
    And amusement at the Father's little joke,
For a novice had been entered for the steeplechasing prize,
    And they found that it was Father Riley's moke!
He was neat enough to gallop, he was strong enough to stay!
    But his owner's views of training were immense,
For the Reverend Father Riley used to ride him every day,
    And he never saw a hurdle nor a fence.

And the priest would join the laughter: "Oh," said he, "I put him in,
    For there's five-and-twenty sovereigns to be won.
And the poor would find it useful, if the chestnut chanced to win,
    And he'll maybe win when all is said and done!"
He had called him Faugh-aballagh, which is French for "clear the course"
    And his colours were a vivid shade of green:
All the Dooleys and O'Donnells were on Father Riley's horse,
    While the Orangemen were backing Mandarin!

It was Hogan, the dog poisoner—aged man and very wise,
    Who was camping in the racecourse with his swag,
And who ventured the opinion, to the township's great surprise,
    That the race would go to Father Riley's nag.
"You can talk about your riders—and the horse has not been schooled,
    And the fences is terrific, and the rest!
When the field is fairly going, then ye'll see ye've all been fooled,
    And the chestnut horse will battle with the best.

For there's some has got condition, and they think the race is sure,
    And the chestnut horse will fall beneath the weight,

But the hopes of all the helpless, and the prayers of all the poor,
    Will be running by his side to keep him straight.
And it's what's the need of schoolin' or of workin' on the track,
    Whin the saints are there to guide him round the course!
I've prayed him over every fence—I've prayed him out and back!
    And I'll bet my cash on Father Riley's horse!"

                    *   *   *

Oh, the steeple was a caution! They went tearin' round and round,
    And the fences rang and rattled where they struck.
There was some that cleared the water—there was more fell in and
        drowned,
    Some blamed the men and others blamed the luck!
But the whips were flying freely when the field came into view,
    For the finish down the long green stretch of course,
And in front of all the flyers—jumpin' like a kangaroo,
    Came the rank outsider—Father Riley's horse!

Oh, the shouting and the cheering as he rattled past the post!
    For he left the others standing, in the straight;
And the rider—well they reckoned it was Andy Regan's ghost,
    And it beat 'em how a ghost would draw the weight!
But he weighed in, nine stone seven, then he laughed and disappeared,
    Like a banshee (which is Spanish for an elf),
And old Hogan muttered sagely, "If it wasn't for the beard
    They'd be thinking it was Andy Regan's self!"

And the poor of Kiley's Crossing drank the health at Christmastide
    Of the chestnut and his rider dressed in green.
There was never such a rider, not since Andy Regan died,
    And they wondered who on earth he could have been.
But they settled it among 'em, for the story got about,
    'Mongst the bushmen and the people on the course,
That the Devil had been ordered to let Andy Regan out
    For the steeplechase on Father Riley's horse!

William Lister Lister, Australia, 1859–1944, *The ever restless sea*, 1892, oil on canvas 122 x 214 cm. Art Gallery of New South Wales. Purchased 1892. Reproduced with the kind permission of William Lister Johnson.

Sunrise on the Coast

Grey dawn on the sandhills—the night wind has drifted
   All night from the rollers a scent of the sea;
With the dawn the grey fog his battalions has lifted,
   At the scent of the morning they scatter and flee.

Like mariners calling the roll of their number
   The sea fowl put out to the infinite deep.
And far overhead—sinking softly to slumber—
   Worn out by their watching, the stars fall asleep.

To eastward where resteth the dome of the skies on
   The sea line stirs softly the curtains of night;
And far from behind the enshrouded horizon
   Comes the voice of a God saying, "Let there be light."

And lo, there is light! Evanescent and tender,
   It glows ruby-red where 'twas now ashen grey;
And purple and scarlet and gold in its splendour—
   Behold, 'tis that marvel, the birth of a day!

Eugène von Guérard, 1811–1901, Australian, *Mount Kosciusko seen from the Victorian Border (Mount Hope Ranges)*, 1866, oil on canvas 107 x 153 cm. Purchased 1870. National Gallery of Victoria, Melbourne.

At the Melting of the Snow

There's a sunny Southern land,
    And it's there that I would be
Where the big hills stand,
    In the South Countrie!
When the wattles bloom again,
    Then it's time for us to go
To the old Monaro country
    At the melting of the snow.

To the East or to the West,
    Or wherever you may be,
You will find no place
    Like the South Countrie.
For the skies are blue above,
    And the grass is green below,
In the old Monaro country
    At the melting of the snow.

Now the team is in the plough,
    And the thrushes start to sing,
And the pigeons on the bough
    Are rejoicing at the Spring.
So come my comrades all,
    Let us saddle up and go
To the old Monaro country
    At the melting of the snow.

The Travelling Post Office

The roving breezes come and go, the reed beds
   sweep and sway,
The sleepy river murmurs low, and loiters on its way,
It is the land of lots o' time along the Castlereagh.

*   *   *

The old man's son had left the farm, he found it dull
   and slow,
He drifted to the great North-west where all the
   rovers go.
"He's gone so long," the old man said, "he's dropped
   right out of mind,
But if you'd write a line to him I'd take it very kind;
He's shearing here and fencing there, a kind of waif
   and stray,
He's droving now with Conroy's sheep along the
   Castlereagh.
The sheep are travelling for the grass, and travelling
   very slow;
They may be at Mundooran now, or past the Overflow,
Or tramping down the black soil flats across by Waddiwong,
But all those little country towns would send the letter wrong,
The mailman, if he's extra tired, would pass them in his sleep,
It's safest to address the note to 'Care of Conroy's sheep'.
For five and twenty thousand head can scarcely go astray,
You write to 'Care of Conroy's sheep along the Castlereagh'."

*   *   *

By rock and ridge and riverside the western mail has gone,
Across the great Blue Mountain Range to take that letter on.
A moment on the topmost grade while open fire doors glare,
She pauses like a living thing to breathe the mountain air,

40

Then launches down the other side across the plains away
To bear that note to "Conroy's sheep along the Castlereagh".

And now by coach and mailman's bag it goes from town to town,
And Conroy's Gap and Conroy's Creek have marked it "further down".
Beneath a sky of deepest blue where never cloud abides,
A speck upon the waste of plain the lonely mailman rides.
Where fierce hot winds have set the pine and myall boughs asweep
He hails the shearers passing by for news of Conroy's sheep.
By big lagoons where wildfowl play and crested pigeons flock,
By campfires where the drovers ride around their restless stock,
And pass the teamster toiling down to fetch the wool away
My letter chases Conroy's sheep along the Castlereagh.

Song of the Wheat

We have sung the song of the droving days,
    Of the march of the travelling sheep;
By silent stages and lonely ways
    Thin, white battlions creep.
But the man who now by the land would thrive
    Must his spurs to a ploughshare beat.
Is there ever a man in the world alive
    To sing the song of the Wheat!

It's west by south of the Great Divide
    The grim grey plains run out,
Where the old flock masters lived and died
    In a ceaseless fight with drought.
Weary with waiting and hope deferred
    They were ready to own defeat,
Till at last they heard the master-word
    And the master-word was Wheat.

Yarran and Myall and Box and Pine—
    'Twas axe and fire for all;
They scarce could tarry to blaze the line
    Or wait for the trees to fall,
Ere the team was yoked and the gates flung wide,
    And the dust of the horses' feet
Rose up like a pillar of smoke to guide
    The wonderful march of Wheat.

Furrow by furrow, and fold by fold,
    The soil is turned on the plain;
Better than silver and better than gold
    Is the surface-mine of the grain.

J. H. Carse, *Harvest Field*, 1870. Collection of the Bendigo Art Gallery, Victoria.

Better than cattle and better than sheep
    In the fight with the drought and heat.
For a streak of stubbornness wide and deep
    Lies hid in a grain of Wheat.

When the stock is swept by the hand of fate,
    Deep down in his bed of clay
The brave brown Wheat will lie and wait
    For the resurrection day:
Lie hid while the whole world thinks him dead;
    But the spring rain, soft and sweet,
Will over the steaming paddocks spread
    The first green flush of the Wheat.

Green and amber and gold it grows
    When the sun sinks late in the West
And the breeze sweeps over the rippling rows
    Where the quail and the skylark nest.

Mountain or river or shining star,
    There's never a sight can beat—
Away to the skyline stretching far—
    A sea of the ripening Wheat.

When the burning harvest sun sinks low,
    And the shadows stretch on the plain,
The roaring strippers come and go
    Like ships on a sea of grain;
Till the lurching, groaning waggons bear
    Their tale of the load complete.
Of the world's great work he has done his share
    Who has gathered a crop of wheat.

Princes and Potentates and Czars,
    They travel in regal state,
But old King Wheat has a thousand cars
    For his trip to the water-gate;
And his thousand steamships breast the tide
    And plough thro' the wind and sleet
To the lands where the teeming millions bide
    That say, "Thank God for Wheat!"

The Man from Snowy River

There was movement at the station, for the word had passed around
That the colt from old Regret had got away,
And had joined the wild bush horses—he was worth a thousand
    pound,
So all the cracks had gathered to the fray.
All the tried and noted riders from the stations near and far
Had mustered at the homestead overnight,

C. Martens (signed, lower right): *View from the Main Dividing Range*, watercolour
19.7 x 29.5 cm. Mitchell Library, Sydney.

For the bushmen love hard riding where the wild bush horses are,
And the stock-horse snuffs the battle with delight.

There was Harrison, who made his pile when Pardon won the cup,
The old man with his hair as white as snow;
But few could ride beside him when his blood was fairly up—
He would go wherever horse and man could go.
And Clancy of the Overflow came down to lend a hand,
No better horseman ever held the reins;
For never horse could throw him while the saddle girths would stand,
He learnt to ride while droving on the plains.

And one was there, a stripling on a small and weedy beast,
He was something like a racehorse undersized,
With a touch of Timor pony—three parts thoroughbred at least—

And such as are by mountain horsemen prized.
He was hard and tough and wiry—just the sort that won't say die—
There was courage in his quick impatient tread;
And he bore the badge of gameness in his bright and fiery eye,
And the proud and lofty carriage of his head.

But so slight and weedy, one would doubt his power to stay,
And the old man said, "That horse will never do
For a long and tiring gallop—lad, you'd better stop away,
Those hills are far too rough for such as you."
So he waited sad and wistful—only Clancy stood his friend—
"I think we ought to let him come," he said;
"I warrant he'll be with us when he's wanted at the end,
For both his horse and he are mountain bred.

"He hails from Snowy River, up by Kosciusko's side,
Where the hills are twice as steep and twice as rough,
Where a horse's hoofs strike firelight from the flint stones every stride,
The man that holds his own is good enough.
And the Snowy River riders on the mountains make their home,
Where the river runs those giant hills between;
I have seen full many horsemen since I first commenced to roam,
But nowhere yet such horsemen have I seen."

So he went—they found the horses by the big mimosa clump—
They raced away towards the mountain's brow,
And the old man gave his orders, "Boys, go at them from the jump,
No use to try for fancy riding now.
And, Clancy, you must wheel them, try and wheel them to the right.
Ride boldly, lad, and never fear the spills,
For never yet was rider that could keep the mob in sight,
If once they gain the shelter of those hills."

So Clancy rode to wheel them—he was racing on the wing
Where the best and boldest riders take their place,

And he raced his stockhorse past them, and he made the ranges ring
With stockwhip, as he met them face to face.
Then they halted for a moment, while he swung the dreaded lash,
But they saw their well-loved mountain full in view,
And they charged beneath the stockwhip with a sharp and sudden dash,
And off into the mountain scrub they flew.

Then fast the horsemen followed, where the gorges deep and black
Resounded to the thunder of their tread,
And the stockwhips woke the echoes, and they fiercely answered back
From cliffs and crags that beetled overhead.
An upward, ever upward, the wild horses held their sway,
Where mountain ash and kurrajong grew wide;
And the old man muttered fiercely, "We may bid the mob good day,
No man can hold them down the other side."

When they reached the mountain's summit, even Clancy took a pull,
It well might make the boldest hold their breath,
The wild hop scrub grew thickly, and the hidden ground was full
Of wombat holes, and any slip was death.
But the man from Snowy River let the pony have his head,
And he swung his stockwhip round and gave a cheer,
And he raced him down the mountain like a torrent down its bed,
While the others stood and watched in very fear.

He sent the flint stones flying, but the pony kept his feet,
He cleared the fallen timbers in his stride,
And the man from Snowy River never shifted in his seat—
It was grand to see that mountain horseman ride.
Through the stringybarks and saplings, on the rough and broken ground,
Down the hillside at a racing pace he went;
And he never drew the bridle till he landed safe and sound,
At the bottom of that terrible descent.

He was right among the horses as they climbed the further hill
And the watchers on the mountain standing mute,
Saw him ply the stockwhip fiercely, he was right among them still,
As he raced across the clearing in pursuit.
Then they lost him for a moment, where two mountain gullies met
In the ranges, but a final glimpse reveals
On a dim and distant hillside the wild horses racing yet,
With the man from Snowy River at their heels.

And he ran them single-handed till their sides were white with foam.
He followed like a bloodhound in their track,
Till they halted cowed and beaten, then he turned their heads for
    home,
And alone and unassisted brought them back.
But his hardy mountain pony he could scarcely raise a trot,
He was blood from hip to shoulder from the spur;
But his pluck was still undaunted, and his courage fiery hot,
For never yet was mountain horse a cur.

And down by Kosciusko, where the pine clad ridges raise
Their torn and rugged battlements on high,
Where the air is clear as crystal, and the white stars fairly blaze
At midnight in the cold and frosty sky,
And where around The Overflow the reed beds sweep and sway
To the breezes, and the rolling plains are wide,
The man from Snowy River is a household word today,
And the stockmen tell the story of his ride.